UNDER THE MERCY

Bakewell Church

UNDER THE MERCY

The poems of Pete Hollingsworth

With an Introduction by
Andrew Francis

THE KETTLE PRESS
Bristol 2015

First published in 2015 by
The Kettle Press, an imprint
of Imagier Publishing
Bristol BS35 3SY
United Kingdom
Email: ip@imagier.com
www.imagier.com

ISBN 13: 978-1-910216-10-1

Cover and text design Allan Armstrong

The paper used in this publication is from a
sustainable source and is elemental chlorine free.

Printed and bound by Booksfactory.co.uk

Contents

Frontis: *Bakewell Church* by Mark Rchards

Preface

Kettle Press is an imprint of Imagier Publishing, dedicated to publishing contemporary 'spiritual' poetry originating in Wessex and the West Country.

At the Kettle Press we acknowledge that all poetry is an intimate expression of a poet's thoughts and reflections on a given subject. This is especially so with spiritual poetry, which has the power to express the most profound thoughts and convey complex feelings in ways that can, in an instant, move the reader or listener into another mode of discernment.

Once published, such intimate creations simultaneously become both personal and public. The private reader is invited to pause, take in each poem and reflect upon it. Publicly, the poems are available beyond the private moment, whether read from a public stage or discussed within a group. In either case engaging with spiritual poetry is not simply an intellectual or metaphysical exercise but a 'spiritual' experience reaching far beyond the mind into the heart and soul of the reader. It is for this purpose the Kettle Press came into being.

Acknowledgements

For a first taste of the power and beauty of poetry, I must thank my father for presenting his rebellious teenage son with Palgrave's 'Golden Treasury' – an act of great optimism! Within it's pages, I discovered wonders and mysteries, and strangely resonant words. Dad – you lit a flame. Amongst many friends who've fanned this flame, the encouragement of Richard Sattin stands out.

Poetry lovers, I suspect, must at some time attempt to express their own thoughts and experiences, and I was no exception. Early attempts are lost (thankfully!), and this volume would not have come into being without the invaluable encouragement of Derek and Geraldine Allchurch. It was through them that the poet Andrew Francis, having seen an early booklet form of 'Under The Mercy', came to give unstintingly of his time and energy advising approaches to publishing. Thank you Derek, Geraldine, and Andrew.

Jean McDonald kindly included 'In Company Of Trees', and 'Looking Over Ludlow' in 'Secret Shropshire' - a recent publication showcasing her fine photography, along with the work of Shropshire artists and poets. Conceived to raise funds for charity, the book sold well. I sent a copy to Andrew Francis who in turn showed it to his publisher Allan Armstrong. I had to 'pinch myself' when I heard that Allan was interested in publishing 'Under The Mercy'! Thank you Allan - I'll always be indebted to your kindness and vision.

Lastly, thanks to my dear wife Gill, whose forbearance during the many times my attention has been 'elsewhere' is gratefully acknowledged.

Pete Hollingsworth

Introduction

I was first introduced to the poetry of Pete Hollingsworth, whilst I was a speaker at the 2012 *Greenbelt* Festival. We began to e-correspond and one thing led to another....

Pete's poetry is enjoyably deceptive in both its innocence and simplicity. For despite the previous inclusion of his verse in locally- or privately-produced regional anthologies[1], this is the first time a solo volume of his work has been published.

It is the task of poets to offer us a vision or question beyond the mere construct of the words. In his book, *The Use of Poetry*, T.S. Eliot posits that Matthew Arnold offers poetry as a surrogate for religion; consider Arnold's 'On Dover Beach' or Eliot's 'The Waste Land'. But poetry is not always a surrogate for religion, as George Herbert or Gerald Manley Hopkins reveal in their work. Much of poetry is about the inward journey as much as any outward experience. The famous words of the imprisoned, Cavalier Poet, Richard Lovelace, remind us of this:

> When love, with unconfined wings, hovers around my face,
> Minds innocent and quiet take, and that for a hermitage....
> If I have freedom in my love and in my thoughts am free,
> Angels alone that soar above enjoy such liberty.[2]

Although, ostensibly a love poem, Lovelace reminds his readers that the expression of freedom of thought and emotion is vital to one's inner humanity. This is never more true than in religious poetry, but in these politically correct days, we may be better to understand it as spiritual poetry. For its very purpose is not to exclusively affirm a religious superstructure but to offer an

---

1   M. Gaunt and P. Waters (ed.) *Secret Shropshire Books,* Ludlow, 2013
2   Richard Lovelace *To Althea from prison* written circa 1642-43

invitation to explore the vision or questions of a spirituality – far beyond the mere construct of the words. Such words may tell of a commonly-shared outward experience but the invitation is to explore the inward journey within the landscape of those words.

The imagery that accompanies and is within Pete's words help us to do this. It is a very English poetry – inspired both by geographical landscape and the metaphorical landscape of an Anglican spirituality.

Poems such as *The Teme,* or *Stroudwater Valleys* are amongst those which tell of the personal landscapes which surround Pete's life, now rooted in the southern Welsh Marches. Yet in each of these areas, the image of the parish church with its spire pointing heavenward is commonplace. It is the very reason for such ecclesiastical architecture – to point to a life that is beyond the ordinary and everyday.

The inward journey of his spirituality, rooted within the life of an Anglican parish, points to that spiritual life which is 'beyond' that can both enrich the ordinary and everyday. Whilst we may not share such an evangelical faith, its' questions are perennial and necessary to those with Peter's own testimony [see his biography on p.98].

Pete's poetry is essentially rhythmic and of a metrical style – almost atypical of much spiritual poetry in many generations. This, combined with his preferred usage of rhyming couplets can, in its manner, take us back to Shakespeare's generation.

Like some traditional hymnody, the reading of these poems requires pause and reflection before moving onto the next. Their innocence and simplicity are deceptive, but they all pose questions, pointing to the vision beyond.

As the popular poet Wendy Cope has proven in just four collections, innocence and simplicity combined with some humour, are a good vehicle for poetry. Recall that she was the BBC's people choice vote in 1998 as the next Poet Laureate and is a favourite English-language poet of the intellectual poet/ bard, Rowan Williams.

Pete poses deep questions which can probe our personal spirituality and human crises, as our lives unfold. To do that within a simplicity of style and everyday language is a gift. To address the big existential questions of the 'life beyond' is part and parcel of the poet's task. One only need think of the Poetry Society President, Jo Shapcott's fourth personal volume, *Of Mutability*[3] about her personal struggle through cancer into remission, to know that the big questions, about life's meaning, are not shunned by the best of contemporary poets. So, again, the 'meaning of life' questions of his work have their place.

Pete Hollingsworth's voice and his poetry are distinctive. Whether you find that voice and verse a comfort or a challenge, you can discover in the subsequent pages. His is a voice and view that will make you ask yourself some serious questions in the quiet spaces of your life. In today's world, that is a gift worth giving some time to.....

Andrew Francis All Saints Day, 2014
Wiltshire

---

3   Jo Shapcott *Of Mutability* London: Faber, 2010

ABANDONMENT

In nineteen eighty-two, our nation was at war
With Argentina, o'er the Falkland Isles
A task force expedition had left England's shore
A voyage of eight thousand miles
To face dangers and hardships and trials

Now four hundred Paras were advancing on Goose Green
And the Argentine barracks in the town
It was the fiercest fighting most of us had seen
Then our Colonel - a soldier of renown
The valiant 'H Jones' was taken down

Two days of ceaseless fighting; ammunition low
We were weary, and hungry, and cold
Our casualties were mounting, and this latest blow
Upon our spirits and our courage told
We knew not what outcome would unfold

I was with Chris Keeble when he assumed command
Upon his face perplexity engraved
The course of this engagement, not as had been planned
Promised little of the victory we craved
Or how our lives and honour might be saved

No military solution could major Keeble find
But he carried about him an old prayer
And seeking to quieten his agitated mind
Gave voice to the words printed there
Abandoning his future to God's care

Then, among the instruments and weapons of war
Our leader understood what he must do
And all the apprehension he'd felt before
Was displaced as his conviction grew
And inward peace and confidence he knew

In the morning briefing his proposal was aired
Surrender terms to offer to our foes
That from further bloodshed we might all be spared
Then off to the Argentines he goes
A white flag of truce above him blows

Meeting his counterparts and talking face to face
Terms were agreed without delay
Fifteen hundred soldiers at the Goose Green base
Conscripted men with small heart for the fray
Surrendered to the Paras that day

A dignified surrender - their national anthem sung
A parade, and the laying down of arms
But Argentine military lethally stung
The repressive ruling junta alarmed
Their ambitions irrevocably harmed

Goose Green marked a turning point for Major Keeble[1] too
Though a glittering career seemed assured
As the 'Prayer of Abandonment' inspires him anew
He campaigns for a nobler reward
To broker peace and help promote accord ❧

---

1   Published with the full consent of Chris Keeble

ALL ABOUT THIS ANCIENT LAND

All about this ancient land
Old redundant churches stand
Dilapidated chapels peer
Past tombs and briers of yesteryear
And buildings, wherein once was heard
The exposition of the Word
Domiciles have now become
Their former function now undone
Or else for commerce they're employed
If not demolished and destroyed

No taste has modern man it seems
For God's approval for his schemes
It enters not into his mind
That God is gracious, patient, kind
And waits with blessings near at hand
To pour them on this faithless land
But modern man will have his way
Won't countenance another's sway
Head bloodied but unbowed he cries
'I'm master of my fate' - and dies... ✎

ARTISTRY

In pastel shades of blue and red and gold
He paints the skies with touches of His glory
See how His skill and artistry unfold
Each morn and eve repeat the wordless story

Oh I have seen the grandeur of great mountains
And rivers white cascading from their heights
And the glow of gardens after summer rains
A world suffused with rainbow colours bright

There is for me, a scene surpassing loveliness
When moonlight plays upon a placid sea
Laying down a causeway of holiness
That I might walk towards eternity

His artistry revives my jaded spirit
Oft troubled with the labours of the day
Joy and reverence in my soul elicit
And gratitude the earth is found this way ❧

ASTONISHMENT

They say he was astonished, how remarkable is that?
The cause of great astonishment, himself so taken back!
Who'd like a god commanded with such authority,
Yet spoken, as no other, with profound simplicity.
Our captain's trusted servant, more family than slave,
Was taken with a fever and must see an early grave -
But the captain'd heard of Jesus, and of his power to heal,
And so sent messengers to him, to make earnest appeal.

Speak as for me, the captain charged,
'You need but say the word,
I too command and men obey, in me is power conferred,
The health of my good servant, is entirely in your hand,
I beg you, in your mercy, to issue your command.
And please do not divert your way by coming 'neath my roof,
For I'm unworthy to receive and fear your just reproof,
The reach of your authority's not bound by time or place,
Nor your compassion limited to those of your own race'.
And when this son of Mary, this scion of David's line,
Received these words, his eye, they say, took on a brighter shine,
As though some kingly treasure, or some great truth he'd found,
'Nowhere', he said, 'in Israel, have I seen such faith abound'.
It seems to me, my brothers, fellow soldiers of Rome,

The confidence the captain showed
had grown from fertile loam:
He understood authority; it's function on the earth,
Yet recognised in Jesus, though of such lowly birth,

A governance transcending that of spirit or of man;
A power supreme and yet benign was walking in the land.
Authority, the like of which, not seen or heard before,
Anointed and compassionate, comfortable, secure.
For the messengers, a promise, gracious and assured,
'From this very moment now, the servant is restored'
When they returned, expectant, unto the captain's door,
It was opened by the servant, as faithful as before.

From then, the captain's household and many of his friends,
Began to follow Jesus; on his promises depend,
As have countless people since, from every land and shore,
Who bow the knee unto the king, and shall do evermore. ❧

BELIEF

People of this bounteous earth, this earth that gave us birth,
For knowledge ever striving, questioning, deriving.
Is all but accident? Was there no prior intent?

Great sun all life sustaining, moon waxing and waning,
Vast stars and constellations, planets at their stations -
In music of the spheres, speech without words we hear.

Every snowflake's unique form, the avalanche and storm,
Northern borealis show, luminescent sea aglow -
Wonders of form and light, inform the inner sight.

Mountains high, and fertile plains, caressed by sun and rains,
Woodlands wild, and forest glades, and meadow flowers arrayed -
Provision for our need: benevolence, we read.

Meerkats, lizards, lions, hares, and terrible great bears,
All beasts of strength and might, all creatures of the night -
Diversity of kind implies a maker's mind.

Birds fluttering and winging, crying, chirping, singing,
Myriad fishes silvery, and all thronging the sea -
How wonderfully you're made: great handiwork displayed.

Butterflies and bumblebees, cicadas in the trees,
Multifarious insects strange, amazingly arranged -
Did chance your limbs align, or intelligent design?

Lakes mysterious; brooding hills, wild waterfalls and rills,
Smooth and stately rivers wide, ebbing and flowing tide -
In loveliness and grace, divinity is traced.

Thoughtful men and women fair, it's ever been our care,
This great world to contemplate: our genesis; our fate!
Is all but accident? Was there no prior intent? ✆

BIRDS OF A FEATHER

The robin red-breast
The bird I like best
Brings such good cheer
When winter is here

The neat jenny wren
Ever now and again
Darts under a shrub
In search of a grub

The bonny blackbird
By danger disturbed
Cries raucous alarm
Keeping others from harm

The busy blue tit
Won't stay still a bit
But swings upside down
For this it's renowned

The cheeky chaffinch
From you won't flinch
If you cast around
Some crumbs on the ground

The speckled song thrush
A snail shell can crush
Or pour melody
Down from a high tree

The strutting starling
When not squabbling
In sunny weather
Preens every feather

Unremarkable sparrows
Old nests may borrow
And chirrup and quip
While rearing their chicks

The lark in the meadow
To mortals below
While high on the wing
Simultaneously sings

The thieving magpie
With a glint in it's eye
In the broad light of day
Steals a bauble away

Wood pigeons a-cooing
When roosting or wooing
If something's the matter
Fly off wings a-clatter

Birds of a feather
A proper endeavour
To know them and love them
Thank heaven above them ❧

COMFORT

In justice, Lord, Your anger flared
For I have many wronged
The mouth of hell before me glared
Where, justly, I belonged

Yet You Your anger turned aside
Remembering the cross
The Lamb upon it, You supplied
At such appalling cost

Yes, You Your anger turned away
One in my place has bled
Mercy oe'r justice won the day
You comfort me instead.

Yes, tenderly, You comfort me
Defend me, as one dear
You strengthen, and assuredly
Calm my anxious fear

And so I raise my voice, compelled
In joyful word and song
The greatness of my God to tell
To whom glory belongs

Let all the world, in every land
In every corner sing
The benefits of His commands
Our Saviour and our King ✆

CRAZY DAY IN NAZARETH

Yes, I was there that crazy day in Nazareth,
The wildest gossip going round the town,
Of how old Joseph's son, the carpenter,
In other towns had healed the blind and bound,
And even those who'd merely touched his gown.
On that awesome Sabbath I was present,
Assembled with the people there to pray;
I saw the sacred scroll of great Isaiah
Handed the young carpenter that day,
When he stood up the reading to relay.

I saw him pause to find where it is written:
'The Spirit of the Lord rests full on me,
For I'm anointed to proclaim good news:
To open sightless eyes, and captives free;
To tell on whom the Lord looks favourably'.
I saw the gaze of all the congregation
Fastened full upon his honest face,
'Today', he said, 'this scripture in your hearing
Has found fulfilment in this time and place'.
And all there marvelled at his words of grace.

But then an evil doubt took root among them,
As on his lowly birth they did reflect,
Which he perceived, and grasping full the nettle,
Condemned their disbelief in words direct:
'No prophet, in his home town finds respect'.
He spoke of those recorded in the scriptures,
Who'd failed to recognise great men of God,

Whose earthbound vision limited experience,
Whose boundaries were but the paths they trod,
Who o'er successive prophets rode roughshod.

And then did Nazareth's fickle congregation
Into a pitiable rabble quickly turn -
Who drove him to the brink of a ravine:
To take his life, it seemed, they would not spurn,
For so intense did mindless anger burn.
Then amazement, compounding amazement,
Scarcely could I trust what I did see,
How impotent all their wrath and rancour:
He passed right through the mob, unharmed and free -
His time to die would be at God's decree.

Yes, I was there that crazy day in Nazareth,
I witnessed all that took place in the town,
No force of arms could discompose Messiah,
His compelling words no storm could drown,
Voluntarily he would his life lay down. ❧

DESPERATION

He took it very well, old Simeon -
The damage they'd inflicted on his roof,
The ragged hole they tore in desperation ,
Which of their care and love was very proof.
Their friend, you see, was terribly disabled,
And needed to be carried everywhere;
They'd heard about the Galilean able
To heal, and broken bodies to repair.

So they'd come, laboriously bearing
The weary invalid upon his bed,
Each man their burden jointly sharing,
As each encouraged each, so hope was fed.
At Simeon's house, the Galilean's teaching
Had drawn from far a crowd, within, without,
Little hope of coming close and reaching
The ear of him they'd heard so much about.

Yes 'twas desperation drove them so,
To hoist their friend up to the roof on high,
And claw makeshift access to the room below,
Let down the bed, the healer standing by.
What a stir this strange descent occasioned,
But the Galilean listened to their plea,
And seeing faith had driven the invasion
Declared, 'Forgiven now your sins shall be'.

You should have seen the looks of consternation,
That precious word 'forgiven' made them smart -
'God alone', they said, 'gives absolution,
He alone forgiveness may impart'.
But the Galilean knew what they were murm'ring,
And with a look of sadness of them asks,
'Of which, to bring healing or forgiving -
Which the most difficult of tasks?'

Then all were filled with wonder, all amazed,
For turning to the man there at his feet,
'Stand up, take up your bed, go home' he says,
At once the man arose healed and complete.
His friends broke into songs of jubilation,
Giving praise and glory unto God,
Then set about the careful restoration,
Of Simeon's roof, where they had lately trod.

Yes, he took it well, old Simeon,
And oft would reminisce with brightened eye.
About his face was written affirmation,
When Jesus in his mercy had stopped by,
He'd entertained the Son of God on high. ❧

DOUGAL and HARRY

When Dougal died quite suddenly
At four and seventy years
A book was found among his things
In which was written clear:

"In token of our friendship,
I'd like to give to you
This testament, whose pages tell
A story great and true
A life at once most beautiful
This world has ever seen
And yet the most heroic
That ever there has been
The words of Jesus, here within
So comfort and inspire
The antidote to doubt and fear
All wisdom we require
No other thing I know of
Can guide our steps each day
As can the words of Jesus
The truth, the light, the way"

Though Dougal kept his teacher's gift
It's pages pristine stayed
And soon his life began to drift
And woes upon him played
But He who conjures deep designs

Whose spirit earth pervades
Honoured the thought behind the gift
As though a prayer was prayed

The hippy mantra, 'Love and Peace'
Caught Harry, Dougal's son
And hedonistic pleasure
Was Harry bent upon
But then he fell for Jesus
The source of Love and Peace
Fell in with Christian people
All trophies of God's grace

That remarkable inscription
Writ in nineteen twenty eight
As last bore fruit in Dougal's life
In nineteen eighty eight:

The day before he fell asleep
Once more God's spirit pleaded
Through gentle words of faithful friend
He found the grace he needed

For that inscribed so long ago
In hand as though God gilden
Was seed that would to fullness grow
In Dougal, and his children[2]. ᖆ

---

2   A good friend recounted this story of his father, and of the inscription
found in the New Testament.

FIGURES ON THE FORESHORE

There are figures on the foreshore of this secluded bay,
Where a Preseli river meets the sea,
Meandering unhurriedly, oft pausing in their way,
Arrested by such tranquillity;

Now stooping to inspect some strange creature of the shore,
Or to brush the sand from bright half buried shells.
The witness of their passing will not for long endure,
Erased by the tide the pale moon swells.

When they have gone, returning to unquiet hurried lives,
They leave no tell tale footprints behind -
Yet something intangible of themselves here survives,
Something of their hearts remains enshrined.

Enshrined amongst the loveliness of this lonely place,
Where the scars of man's endeavours are few,
Where insistent wordless whispers proclaim 'glory and grace',
And all with wonder glistens like the dew.

So few will leave a trace on earth of their existence here,
Of benefice, or notoriety:
The tide of time obliterates, we mostly disappear;
Sparse words upon a stone our history.

Is life then meaningless as some hasten to say?
Leave we no lasting patterns in the sands?
The risen one of Calvary knows no such dismay -
Nor his followers, their names writ on his hands. ❧

HALLELUJAH

I heard there was a secret chord,
That you played and it pleased the Lord,
And turned the ear of Israel's King unto ya:
Such music as must all enthral,
Soothed the troubled soul of Saul,
This yielding of the tongue to Hallelujah.
Hallelujah, Hallelujah, Hallelujah, Hallelujah.

You gathered pebbles from a brook,
Goliath's head you bravely took,
Trusting all the while the Hallelujah.
The Lord's anointed you became,
King David now your royal name,
And still the music pleased all those who knew ya.
Hallelujah, Hallelujah, Hallelujah, Hallelujah

You left the battle, stood aloof,
Saw her bathing from the roof,
Her beauty and the moonlight overthrew-ya.
Besotted by Bathsheba's eyes,
Arranged Uriah's swift demise,
Yet reckoned you could still sing Hallelujah.
Hallelujah, Hallelujah, Hallelujah, Hallelujah

A poor man's lamb loved as a daughter,
A wealthy tyrant stole for slaughter,
The prophet Nathan told this story to-ya.
You were angered at such greed,
Death, you said, should reward the deed,
And Nathan raised a pointed finger though-ya.
Hallelujah, Hallelujah, Hallelujah, Hallelujah

Oh hear the words that Nathan cried,
'The Lord has laid your sin aside',
But now the sorrows of the sword shall rue-ya.
You'll tear your clothes and weep in vain,
Then rise, and raise your voice again,
In worship of the Lord: the Hallelujah.
Hallelujah, Hallelujah, Hallelujah, Hallelujah

For David, from your royal line,
Will come a King in God's own time,
Whose spirit even now is moving through ya.
A lamb, a shepherd, priest and friend:
Jesus' reign will never end,
All earth sings universal Hallelujah!
Hallelujah, Hallelujah, Hallelujah, Hallelujah ✍

HE CHANGED PLACES

Long ago in Palestine a sad man lived apart,
Cast out from society, in loneliness and poverty,
In sickness and infirmity, and brokenness of heart.
Then into this darkness there came a shining light
And hope was newly woken,
'Will You cleanse this body broken?'
The words, 'I will', were spoken
And darkness took to flight.

He changed places, compassionately,
He changed places: decay for purity.
He changed places - again upon that tree,
He changed places, He changed places,
He changed places...for you, and for me.[3] ✎

---

3   A reflection on Luke 5:12

IN CASE WE SHOULD CALL

We don't need to dial His number,
We don't need to text His phone,
Neither an address for email,
We don't need to check He's home.
No need of a powerful transmitter,
No need for a megaphone:
For His ear is ever open,
Listening, in case we should call;
Through the Son, the barrier's broken,
The river of His mercy flows for all.

No need to travel a great distance,
Or make out an application form,
No need to plead for an audience,
Or with some protocol conform.
We don't need to pay for the privilege,
No seeker will ever be scorned:
For His ear is ever open,
Listening, in case we should call;
Through His Son, the barrier's broken,
The river of His mercy flows for all. ❧

IN COMPANY OF TREES

In the wilderness of winter, when nature's gone to ground
Lowlands are flooded, sunlight filters down
I'll wander in the byways, once again to see
The tracery and form of winter's trees

In the wakening that follows winter's weary night
When everything's responsive to the catalyst of light
I'll wander in the country, once again to see
The fresh unfolding foliage of trees

Through changing seasons
                Ease is given me
                        In company of trees

In the drowsiness of summer, when watercourses dry
And cattle seek for shelter from an overbearing sky
I'll follow forest footpaths, once again to be
Beneath the canopy of trees

In 'mists and mellow fruitfulness', the earth we hold dear
Has yielded up her harvest: the crowning of the year
I'll walk among the woodlands, once again to see
The pageantry and colours of trees

Through changing seasons
                Ease comes to me
                        In company of trees
                                In the glory and gracefulness of trees ❧

IN THE GARDEN

When came the fading of the light
It was his practice to repair
Unto a garden, and delight
In reverential prayer;
And of his father's table fare,
And in communion with him share.

His footsore followers, lingering near,
In muted tones review the day.
Arrested now by what they hear,
They eavesdrop as their master prays.
They see him fall, they hear him weep,
Then in their weariness, they sleep.

And now the awful hour draws nigh,
As beads upon his brow attest.
Impassioned prayer and anguished cry:
Was ever virtue so oppressed?
'Your will on earth be done', he pleads,
See, that great heart of love, it bleeds!

Black night of darkness closes in,
Guttering torches smoke and sway;
Uneasy soldiers ,muttering:
Infernal schemes abhor the day.
A eerie coldness clings, and this:
Friendship betrayed - a sordid kiss.

A brief interrogation:
He asks them who they seek.
An awesome proclamation:
'I am', to whom you speak.
And that invested in his name,
Compels their falling, as the slain.

The scene is re-enacted,
The dialogue repeats,
But status is retracted -
He yields to their conceits.
Swords were never needed,
His life he has conceded.

The Lamb is for the slaughter bound
Upon a rough hewn timber cross -
Where you and I will gather round,
With all our selfishness and dross.
We'll mock, and spit, and curse him there:
'Father, forgive', is all his care,

And, hung upon the torture tree,
Waves of pain engulf him now.
For his tormentors – sympathy,
For them the thorns upon his brow.
For he has made a pact to give
His life to death, that we may live.

Before the bowing of his head,
High and exultant is the cry -
The task of which he'd lain in dread
Is finished: he prepares to die.
And as the earth in wonder shakes,
The veil within the temple breaks.

And in a garden now they lay
His embalmed body in a tomb -
But angels roll the stone away:
He rises from the earthly womb!
And death, the last great enemy
Is swallowed up in victory.

That brutal instrument of pain,
Of all devices the most cruel,
Now hangs upon a silver chain
And elevated to a jewel.
No greater symbol now of love,
No greater sign of heaven above.

As life is subject to the sun
Whose rays supply our mortal needs,
His subjects look unto the one
Who with the father intercedes:
The crucified and lowly lamb,
Their mighty king, the great 'I am'. ✺

INSIGHT

Beside the road there, sitting in the shade,
Together we would pass the time of day.
We heard the nearby children as they played,
And marked the talk of travellers on the way.
We loved the cadences and calls of birds,
The cheerful cicadas in the trees,
The calls of distant shepherds too, we heard,
Carried o'er the fields upon the breeze.

All sounds, to us, were windows on the world,
Our ears acute to every nuanced note.
We felt attuned to truth when such we heard,
Or the fishbone of deceit within the throat.
Sometimes we'd call to those who journeyed by,
Whose conversation fell upon our ear,
And ask to know the reason why they sighed -
What news they had of joy, of hope, of fear.

And we had time to weigh the tales they weaved,
And to debate the import of their news.
Perhaps, unseeing, yet we well perceived,
And with a clear discernment formed our views.
Now for a year of more of one we'd heard,
A Nazarene, whose teaching lit a flame;
Whose wondrous deeds had greatly stirred
And warmed the hearts of many to his name.

My friend and I would dwell upon each story,
Each anecdote or rumour, we were told,
Of this son of Joseph and of Mary:
Could he be the one so long foretold?
Came the day we learnt he might pass by,
Of this we babbled on like any child,
We hoped the one Isaiah prophesied,
Had come that man to God be reconciled.

The growing noisy clamour of a crowd,
The oft repeated calling of his name:
We stood and waved and shouted out aloud,
Although the crowd would silence us, for shame.
We cried, as only drowning men might cry,
'Have mercy on us, Son of David, Lord!'
And then we felt his touch upon our eyes,
Immediately our sight was thus restored!

So his the face that first we looked upon,
His the features first our eyes impressed:
We never would forget how his face shone,
Or how his presence intimated rest.
Rejoicing, we followed him that day,
And saw his vast compassion for the crowd,
How for each needy soul he would delay,
How he with grace and truth was so endowed.

Though days of deepest darkness lay ahead,
We lived to see his greatest triumph won.
The crown of thorns that pierced messiah's head,
Become a crown of glory like the sun. ❧

JERICHO ROAD

Nathan knew the risk of such a journey,
From Jerusalem, alone, to Jericho;
But his was an errand of mercy,
For the sake of an old friend he had to go.
So setting out he made at first good progress,
Passing workers toiling in the fields,
But the road descended into barrenness,
And places desperate men might lie concealed.

Then, with more than half the journey covered,
Nathan sensed he now was not alone,
He felt the presence of some unseen other:
Quickened his pace, thought fondly of home.
At once a figure bearing club and dagger,
Appeared before him, clearly boding ill,
He fell to unseen blows that made him stagger,
He knew then robbers had him at their will.

They seized upon his little food and money,
They seemed incensed he did not carry more,
They took his clothes and beat upon him sorely,
Left him as for dead in pain and gore.
Then, drifting in and out of consciousness,
Where he had fallen there beside the road,
He thought he saw one pass, compassionless:
A priest, in whom more fear than pity flowed.

He saw the shadows lengthen, night drew on,
Again, a traveller came by where he lay;
But onwards passed towards his destination,
Too important was his purpose for delay.
Now cold of eve induced a weary numbness,
He doubted he would see another day;
He thought of those with whom he'd known a oneness,
Who'd mourn his passing there beside the way.

When he came round, amidst surreal surroundings,
A room swept clean, bathed in warmth and light,
And saw around his wounds white bandagings -
Had some angel pitied his sore plight?
It was no dream, no fantasy of heaven,
And there, beside the bed he rested on,
With bread and wine and olives, laden,
A table stood - for him to eat upon.

In the days that led to his recovery,
He knew his host as keeper of an inn,
His saviour, though, remained beyond discovery,
Who had paid for his sojourn within?
Nathan learnt one detail of this mystery:
In later years a stranger passing near
Told the parable of the Good Samaritan:
Nathan's own story fell upon his ear. ❧

KINGDOM

They came to Ellis Island in their millions,
Seeking new life among the free,
A land wherein was valued each civilian,
A land of hope and opportunity,

They'd turned their backs on their native countries,
Where oppression or prejudice held sway;
Some came alone; some, penniless, in families -
They came to labour, pioneer, and pray.

No new lands remain now still uncharted,
No virgin shore, nor some untrodden lea,
No haven for the brave or broken hearted,
No new worlds across the open sea.

What dream now for all the disenchanted,
Who for the indefinable yearn?
Desperation with bright hope supplanted;
To what new world today may seekers turn?

There's yet a land, a realm, a unique kingdom,
And pilgrim souls still sail unto its shores,
They come as new-born children of salvation,
Forgiven and rejoicing and restored.

If we should make this land our destination;
Care to join it's subjects in their joy -
We need to cross the waters of delusion;
The Way of Truth and Light we must employ.

We'll need no chart or compass, but a person;
A guide and captain, who knows the way,
One who needs no payment or persuasion,
Available to all this very day:

'Come', he says to all the heavy laden;
'Come all who walk today in doubt or fear,
For I will take upon myself your burden,
And you, to Heaven's Kingdom, I will steer.

Come board my ship, her name is Redemption,
At the quay of Forgiveness she is found,
Her anchor, my every word and sentence;
To the Kingdom Heaven she is bound'.

The journey to this Kingdom can't be measured
As a distance, or in passing of time;
For this land is spiritually treasured
In feast of broken bread and holy wine' ❧

LIGHT IN THE DARKNESS

Darkness adroitly as light masquerades,
In guise of wisdom darkness parades;
Minds that on vengeance and violence dwell,
Are farthest from heaven, and closest to hell;.
Sadistic violence, screened for our sport,
Engenders darkness and reason distorts;
In cities subject to disorder and fear
The innocent suffer in sorrow and tears;
If minds filled with darkness have access to guns,
Fear for our daughters and fear for our sons:
In confusion of darkness we stumble and fall -
Blind leading the blind! Lord pity us all

How precious, how lovely, the nature of light,
Investing with beauty, enabling sight;
From flower of the meadow to sky's vast array,
Light glorifying the otherwise grey;
There's a light illumines and nurtures the mind,
Light with compassion and wisdom aligned;
The brother of Truth and sister of Right,
Vanquishing darkness, banishing night -
This glorious light our reason informs,
With insight and vision our spirit adorns:
In composure and peace we follow the way,
Your light Lord provides, lest we go astray. ❧

LUDLOW

Looking over Ludlow at the rising of the sun
From the hill above the river where the silver salmon run
A rosebud unfolding, it's petals soon undone
In beauty and innocence the day has just begun

Looking down on Ludlow from the high church tower
As the clock chimes and counts down the noontide hour
In the market, the cheery, the deft, and the dour
The caring, the cursing, the sweet and the sour

Looking beyond Ludlow from the ancient castle wall
To Clee hill and to Clun, as the evening shadows fall
Commerce is quieted, distant curlews call
Forgive us our trespasses, forgive us all ✎

MARTHA and MARY

Martha, Oh Martha, you're troubled I see
While your sister Mary just sits at my knee
The heat of the kitchen, so much to prepare
And you don't consider it fair
You question if I even care

You've opened your house, and greeted each guest
So precious your name as a gracious hostess
By detail distracted, with worry oppressed
But Mary has chosen what's best

There once was a merchant, fine pearls his desire
His treasured collection widely admired
But all his possessions he sold to acquire
One pearl of perfection entire
One pearl of perfection entire

All else, to the value of hearing my voice
Is little more than distraction
Mary has made me the pearl of her choice
And she must not suffer detraction

Martha, Oh Martha, you're troubled I see
While your sister Mary sits at my knee
Your labour is valued, you also are blessed
But Mary has chosen what's best
But Mary has chosen what's best[4] ❧

---

4   Based on Luke 10:38-42, and Matthew 13: 45-46

MICHAL

It met your disapproval then this dancing,
The king, disrobed, in all the peoples' sight;
This outrageous spectacle of prancing:
Israel's king gyrating in delight.

This David, this man of strength and valour,
Who you once looked upon with doleful eyes,
Gives offence, with all his zeal and fervour,
And in your heart, your husband you despise.

But you had never been one to worship
This Yahweh, this great God of Abraham;
His rules and regulations a hardship,
Your compliance little more than sham.

You had always been acutely conscious
Of your high royal status and descent;
Your wealth and privilege so precious,
So David's self abasement you resent.

Now your contempt, public and outspoken,
Confirms in David that which he had feared;
His union with you, henceforth, is broken -
Complaint and gratitude cannot adhere.

David's name will evermore be honoured,
While yours, associated hence with shame;
His passionate outpourings ever treasured,
While pride and childlessness stain your name.

Did he care for you as you both grew older?
Concerned for the softening of your heart;
At last did you cry upon his shoulder
Acknowledging his the nobler part?[5] ❧

5   Based on 2 Samuel 6:16

MUSTARD SEED

Amongst the smallest things, in those days to be seen:
A tiny mustard seed, so commonplace a thing;
It was the largest mass - the contrast so extreme -
Mountain vastness seen alone by eagles on the wing.

And so it is with faith, with trust in God above:
In His compassion, care, and fatherly love.
Even if such faith, like mustard seed is small,
He rejoices in our trust - the mountain must fall.

When challenges arise that would obstruct the way;
When problems are encountered, that will not go away -
If familiar with his word, faith we may employ
To rest in his providence, and his power enjoy. ❧

NATHANIEL

What are you doing Nathaniel,
Sitting yet again beneath this tree?
Have you nothing better to be doing?
You should use your time more usefully!
Must you always be such a dreamer?
Why can't you help more round the house?
Since you've taken up with that wild preacher,
Sometimes I wish I was not your spouse!

And why so much talk about this Jesus:
All he does and all you've heard him say?
Can't you see it will end in trouble?
Authorities will always have their way.
Since you've joined Jesus's followers -
And what motley riff raff they are -
Simple fishermen, some tax collector:
Your behaviour has become quite bizarre!

This Jesus, you say, comes from Nazareth;
Can any good come from such a town?
Yet you say he's the one expected,
And you'd place upon his head a crown.
How can you put so much faith in him;
Does he really command such respect?
Because he said he saw you 'neath this tree?
Oh why can't you be more circumspect?

I'm sorry, dear, you find this irksome;
I'm sorry my devotions give you pain -
But I've seen the very heavens open,
Angels attending Jesus again:
Let me ask once more, come and meet him,
Hear his words and look into his face -
For I wish that all the world would greet him;
All the world, this Jesus, would embrace.[6] ❧

6   Based on John 1: 43-51

NATURE

Sun shining down on the meadow
Dappled light falling through trees
A flash of bright wings in the hedgerow
Such sights are sweetness to me

Moonlight falling on mountains
Or casting a path on the sea
The stars above beyond counting
Such scenes are lovely to me

White rolling surf on the seashore
The wingbeat of swans o'er the lea
The lark's incomparable measure
Such sounds are precious to me

All the provision of nature
On earth, in the sea, and the skies
Such blessings ever enrapture
My spirit heavenwards flies ❧

NO ORDINARY JOE

He'd seen her playfulness and easy grace,
And marked her gentleness and growth apace,
And how her smile would linger on her face:
Mary's love he sought to know,
Mary's love he sought to know.

She loved to see the wood beneath his hand,
Take shape and form as at his wise command,
And his well chosen words her feelings fanned:
He was no ordinary Joe,
He was no ordinary Joe.

So each unto the other did declare,
Steadfast Joseph and maid Mary fair,
To love and cherish and in all things share:
Unto the church they soon should go,
Unto the church they soon should go.

We make our plans and lay our little schemes,
And fret and toil to realise our dreams,
A brooding spirit on our enterprises leans:
Mary with child! Joe last to know,
Mary with child! Joe last to know!

Betrayed! Betrayed! She must be weak and base,
Yet Joe, you seek to shield her from disgrace,
And though perplexity has marked your face:
Your love is greater than your woe,
Your love is greater than your woe! ❧

An angel in your dreams your fears relieve:
'Honour Mary, Joe; marry and believe
By brooding Spirit is the child conceived,
In Mary's womb, Immanuel grows!
In Mary's womb, Immanuel grows'.

Thus is fulfilled what was of old foretold,
Man's awful enmity with God resolved,
The case against us through Jesus is dissolved:
Mercy and grace unto us flows,
Mercy and grace unto us flows. ❧

NOT UNLIKE AN ANGEL

Wherein more beauty, we suppose,
Than in an angel's face -
Where light and joy and peace repose
In purity and grace.
So few on earth have been allowed
An angel's face to see -
And yet our spirits are endowed
To view such symmetry.

No trace of pride, or anxious care,
Mar an angel's features;
Of their own beauty unaware -
Holy ageless creatures.
We lesser mortals are at pains
Appearances to fashion:
Such endeavours vain remain,
Betrayed by our passions.

Our troubled and unruly souls
Etch on our brows deep furrows;
We entertain ignoble goals,
Then reap sheaves of sorrow.
Our features, bright with youth's first bloom,
Like dew upon the rose,
Are cast and sullied all too soon
By self inflicted woes.

And yet is seen the human face,
Some with years full seasoned,
Aglow with brush strokes of God's grace:
With His love envisioned.
In worship lost...and found... and free,
To in His mercy dwell -
And beautif'lly, remarkably,
Not unlike an angel. ✒

PETER

Why is the cockerel crowing
So long before sunrise?
Why are you bitterly weeping,
Why so swollen your eyes?

What now of your grand avowal
To be by his side come what may?
You know he foresaw this betrayal:
You knew not yourself 'till this day.

You cannot bear to be watching
This scene upon Golgotha hill.
He in whom you'd been trusting
From his writhing soon will be still...

So this must be a conclusion -
Such intolerable suffering and pain;
A Roman and Jewish collusion,
Whom you thought messiah is slain...

Three days, this mover and shaker
Has lain cold in a stone sealed grave;
This deluded or mad troublemaker,
Saved others, himself could not save.

Peter, why are you running
With such unseemly haste?
Surely Mary was dreaming -
Such a stone could not be displaced.

What at his grave are you seeking;
What, in his tomb, you have found?
Of what are the grave-clothes speaking?
Who folded the cloth his head bound?

Why in fear are you staying
Behind doors bolted and barred?
Who appears, his body displaying,
So wounded and terribly scarred?

Peter, why go you fishing -
To find solace in old routines?
And why no fish are you catching:
Is failure still haunting your schemes?

Who is on the shore calling?
Is that his familiar voice?
The one who predicted your falling?
Forgiveness was always his choice!

Why does he ask the same question:
A thrice repeated refrain?
You're witness to his resurrection!
You will never deny him again! ✺

PRODIGAL

As I look back, in later years at all the harm I'd done,
The wonder grows my father should still call me his son.
I'd always been rebellious, always wanted more:
To drain the cup of pleasure; consume the apples core.
Life at home was so mundane, the city lights so bright -
So I'd asked my father to advance my birthright.
I'd not expected his consent - thought he would be outraged,
But he was wise, my father, he loosed me from my cage.

So in haste I took my leave, oblivious to his pain,
Seeing only pleasure, my new found wealth would gain.
I took the road to distant lands, light-hearted on the way,
If pleasures cost, no matter - I had the means to pay.
In liberal handed revelry I gathered friends with ease;
To every urge I yielded, no thrill I did not seize.
But one by one each pleasure paled - at length I would discern:
Increasing indulgence gave diminishing return.

A gnawing sense of emptiness took root within my soul;
Hollow grew the pleasures that once had been my goal.
Such wayward dissipation took toll upon my health,
Eroded my resources, came poverty by stealth.
I had to find the means to live - my friends against me turned;
No skills had I to offer, no profession learned.
By day: a pittance labouring - the gutters now I swept;
By night: a dreary subway the room in which I slept.

And all the while, I came to know, my father, every day,
Lived in hope that I'd return, and for this he would pray;
That he would gaze at evening, way down the dusty track,
Never once despairing that one day I'd come back.
Then came a night when I was robbed - what irony in this:
As I was all but penniless they thought me much remiss,
So, viciously, they worked their will, and beat me to the ground,
As though some punishment, deserved, for being meanly found.

Yet looking back, I feel I'd thank each sorry soul by name,
For though they beat me senseless, to my senses then I came;
I thought about my father's staff - his faithful employees -
Who though not rich, yet nothing lacked, if not of want, of need.
I reasoned thus, and turned my steps towards the place once home,
To of my father's mercy beg, if he'd not me disown:
With this resolve, I journeyed long, but at length, drawing near,
My courage faded with each step - rejection greatly feared.

I had rehearsed the words I'd use, when we came face to face,
But now, no words seemed adequate, to mitigate disgrace;
And when at last I caught a glimpse of my old home ahead,
With leaden heart, I turned around, to walk away instead.
And then it was I thought I heard a voice I knew so well;
I fancied that it called my name, though I could hardly tell -
I turned again, and now I saw, to my intense surprise,
My father, running with great haste, no doubting now his cries.

I saw the moisture in his eyes as he now drew abreast,
He spoke my name, again, again, no other word expressed
The bursting fervour of his joy - he held me to his breast;
And I would then have bared my soul and all my fault confessed -
But he with fatherly concern, bid my tongue at rest.
He drew me to my feet from where I'd fallen, guilt oppressed;
No force of arms, no evil art, from his strong arms could wrest
This wayward son; this wanton one, undeservedly so blessed.

I saw my father's character that day in a new light:
How outrageous his love for me, how unfeigned his delight
That I'd returned, as from the grave, once more upon his sight.
Casting aside my rags of shame, he clothed me all in white.
He gave direction that same day: celebration must begin -
Some though were offended, even one of my own kin,
Indignant that such welcoming was not just or right -
But patiently he won them round: 'My son's alive, contrite!'

As I look back, in later years at all the harm I'd done,
The wonder grows my father should still call me his son. ൞

QUANDARY

Were I constant and true
Trustworthy in all I do
He might allow unto me
More of himself to see

Were I honest and fair
And all deceit forswear
Heaven he might show
To me on earth below

Were I gentle and kind
Free from selfish design
Then he might let me stay
Close by him day by day

Were I peaceful and pure
All prejudice abjure
He might permit me sight
Of his radiance bright

It comes, O lord, to this
In all I am remiss
Discipleship I see
Does not come easily

Oh, help me in my quest
Your spirit on me rest
My best endeavours bless
And use me nonetheless ❧

REGULATION

There's rules and regulation for everything today.
Bureaucracy oe'r living has official sway;
We have to have a licence for most of what we do;
Application must be made in black ink, not in blue.

And if there's some anomaly not covered by the book,
Your governmental bureaucrat won't take a second look -
If, that is, you can connect with a human voice,
To ask that common sense, for once, might drive official choice.

Prohibition notices proliferate around,
Even in the countryside, increasingly, are found:
'No Picnicking', 'No Swimming' - someone might be hurt,
And sue the local council who must remain alert.

And though we smile and shake our heads, simultaneously,
There's a fundamental problem affecting you and me:
As regulation multiplies and restriction runs rife -
So lessens opportunity for meaningful life.

But regulation and restraint must accompany
The intercourse of nations, of man, of you and me:
Inured in selfishness and greed, too ready to accuse,
We, for our own purposes, extort, deceive, abuse.

Ten simple regulations, passed down from age to age,
Were never meant to 'spoil the fun' - though some against them rage;
They form a firm foundation, for justice and for peace;
Were they but embraced by all, our troubles all would cease.

Even these have been reduced from ten to only two,
By one who's words have touched the hearts of men the ages through.
Two great commandments, at once simple and profound:
The love of God and neighbour - by these alone be bound!

This world pretends allegiance to the second of these laws:
To love our neighbours as ourselves - a celebrated cause!
But evidence on every hand confirms reality:
Man's inhumanity to man is normality.

And the first commandment, 'Love God wholly from the heart,
With mind and soul and strength - totality, not part',
So many judge irrelevant or the order would invert:
'Philanthropy is paramount' so many would assert.

Yet to honour our fellow men, to love them as we should,
With justice and compassion, to serve our neighbours good;
To do unto others as we'd have them do to us,
Is practiced too infrequently - we are impoverished thus.

For we must be enabled if we are to succeed
In caring, not just for our own, but for another's need;
Enabled by God's spirit; descending as a dove,
Bearing witness to Jesus - the embodiment of love.

Intimacy with the God, who gave his own dear son,
Is wholly indispensible for each and every one
Who'd live in a community, both peaceful and free -
Bound not by regulation, but caring harmony. ❧

RESPONSE

How respond the wind and waves to his command, 'Be still!'
They cease their wanton fury, obedient to his will.

How respond the children in their simplicity?
In the balm of his presence, they sit upon his knee.

How respond the fishermen of lake Galilee?
They leave their nets and follow, disciples they would be.

How responds the rabbis, in whom wisdom may be found?
The light of Jesus' teaching, the rabbis all astound.

How respond the lawyers who'd put him to the test?
The discernment of his answers leave them all speechless.

How responds the woman who walks at night the street?
Seeing love incarnate, with tears she bathes his feet.

How respond the villagers who learn he's passing near?
They gather all around him, his words seeking to hear

How responds Peter to so great a catch of fish?
'I am a sinful man, Lord, depart from me', his wish.

How respond the temple guards with orders to arrest?
'No man ever spoke like him', together they attest.

UNDER THE MERCY

How responds the centurion to his dying words?
'This man was the son of God', the soldier averred.

How responds dead Lazarus to his command, 'Come out?
Miraculously he obeys; for death is put to rout!

How respond the disciples on the Emmaus road?
They recognise the risen Lord, as their hearts glowed

How do we respond to him, and all that he proclaimed?
Are our opinions second hand, by others subtly framed?

Or do we prevaricate, or view him with distain?
Or examine the evidence, and weigh his great claims? ✤

SHE BATHES HIS FEET

She bathes his feet,
This sullied broken woman of the street,
She bathes his feet.
With fragrance rare,
With warm and contrite tears of tender care,
And with her hair, with her hair.

Sorrow and joy,
Twin fountains of the tears she employs,
Sorrow and joy.
He sees how bruised
Her features and her soul so long abused -
Now love infused, love infused

His gracious face,
Looks down in mercy, blind to her disgrace,
Sees her as chaste.
And he declares,
Forgiven all the ways in which she's erred,
Her life repaired, life repaired.

He bathes their feet,
Removes the baseless grounds of their conceit,
He bathes their feet.
We bathe his feet
When we another's needs in mercy meet,
We bathe his feet. ✋

SOLDIERS OF ROME

Slept they, I wonder, easily those soldiers who had nailed
His unresisting figure to those beams;
Had they no care or pity for the one they thus impaled?
Did Golgotha thereafter haunt their dreams?

Had they briefly caught his eye, as they prepared to strike,
And been distracted by the candour of his gaze;
Heard they again the ringing of the hammers on each spike -
Could the memory of that scene not be erased?

And did they come to realise their labour that day
In the history of violence stands unique;
Did they understand Emanuel gave his life away,
Did they recall the words they heard him speak?

In extraordinary silence, for the most part he'd hung -
On the few words he uttered we might dwell.
No rage or retribution, no curses from his tongue -
But compassion from an everlasting well.

And as they sat in huddled groups about those crosses three,
Those soldiers wearied of malicious sport,
Were they ill at ease and fractious in such proximity
Of the one who for their sakes his life cut short?

Did they hear those treasured words: his petition voiced in pain
On behalf of his abusers gathered there;
Did they, by his sacrifice, their own forgiveness gain -
Might these soldiers also in his mercy share?

UNDER THE MERCY

I wonder, slept they easily, all who'd cruelly railed
Against the lamb in whom Pilate found no fault:
The priests and the people who ironically had hailed
As king, who so many now exalt?

The soldiers, priests, and people - this unruly ugly crowd
Who'd bayed for his blood in vacuous spite -
Did their words themselves discomfort, like a dark lowering cloud,
Dismaying them in watches of the night?

Did some seek absolution and, not knowing where to turn,
Mouth a hesitant penitent prayer
To the very one who's teaching they'd been so quick to spurn
And found how quick is his forgiving care? ℘

SOMETHING ABOUT JESUS

There's something about Jesus, it's hard to deny,
Something clear and beautiful that begs the question why -
In all recorded history His impact is unique -
Why still today so many of his great passion speak.

There's something about Jesus that sets him apart,
Something deep and wonderful that touches the heart;
There's no other teaching, nor man's philosophy,
So answers our hungers and quiets anxiety.

There's something about Jesus, so many have declared,
Something rich and valuable, that has to be shared;
The joys of his companionship so greatly outweigh,
The wild pursuit of pleasures which last but for the day.

There's something about Jesus, trustworthy and true;
Something of antiquity, something wholly new -
Contemplation of his claims, in each successive age,
Has ennobled the minds of all who with him engage.

There's something about Jesus that causes some offence,
Something pure and faultless that irks self confidence;
His teachings don't sit easily with the proud and vain,
Who ridicule his followers, Him crucify again.

There's something about Jesus inexpressibly divine:
Authority and gentleness sweetly intertwined.
So today, around the earth, His praises never cease;
Vast numbers of his worshipers continue to increase. ❧

STORM

So placid was the lake before the storm,
Before the wind came on it's surface beating:
Aroused its waters to such form
As sent each sailor's courage fleeting.

For several craft had ventured far from shore,
And lives seemed not long for the keeping -
Yet one the tumult did ignore,
Astern upon a pillow sleeping.

Composed in sleep as though a child
Safe and secure within a parent's caring -
A wonder this among waves so wild,
While all were fearful and despairing.

Then he, awakened by the urgent plea,
'Care you not we perish drowning?'
Arises, and in majesty,
Addresses nature's forces raging:

'Be still', he says, 'be now at peace' -
The wind and waves his voice obeying,
Soon their tortured foaming cease:
Smoothed waters mirror the moon's rising.

And as the fear of death fades away,
The wayward wind softly sighing -
Apprehension yet holds sway:
His very presence terrifying!

Who is this man whose spoken word
Overrules nature, souls saving?
His the voice creation heard:
The engine of creation's being.

He is the Word come down as man;
In guise of man is God appearing.
The Prince of Peace, the great I Am -
Entirely worthy our revering.

Placid Lake Galilee again.
Turmoil ceases at his calming.
All in allegiance to his reign
Find peace above this world's alarming. ❧

THE EAR OF HEAVEN

A bright young lark, and weathered crow
Decided they to church should go
To lift in song their voices high
Unto the Lord of earth and sky

At first the lark began to sing
As though to make the rafters ring
And many a wondrous soaring note
Came pouring from it's avian throat

But when the crow took up the air
In tone and time bereft of flair
The lark abruptly ceased it's song
Such raucous praise, it felt all wrong

'How disappointed', thought the lark
'Must be the Lord, to have to hark
To this cacophony of noise
Devoid of all my tuneful poise'

The minister – a wise old owl
Was sad to see the lark so scowl
But thought the feathers of the crow
With luminescence seemed to glow

The Lord, he knew, would take delight
In music lauding truth and light
But, greater far than music's claim
Loves adoration's pure refrain

The weathered crow cawed from it's heart
To heaven's ear, the sweetest art
The lark, for all it's skilled finesse
Made sound to heaven savourless ❧

STROUDWATER VALLEYS

Sheepscombe and Bisley, Chalford and Slad
The villages Laurie Lee knew as a lad
Along beech wooded valley and hazel flanked steams
Though from you I've wandered, of you I still dream

Shy Cotswold cottages scattered and strewn
Bathed in the sunlight, washed by the moon
Tucked in your hillsides, organically grown
Of local timer and close quarried stone

Well tended gardens where row upon row
Show-worthy vegetables flourish and grow
Rose-rambled lintels o'er left open doors
To neighbour or stranger a welcome assures

Wild flowers in profusion adorn the old ways
Of shepherd and drover and children at play
Primroses, cowslips, the scabious blue
Throng hollows where lovers vow to be true

Chickens for eggs, bacon from sows
Sheep for the wool, cream from the cows
The form and the function of your great barns
Attest to the bounty of field and of farms

Sapperton, Nympsfield, Uley and Cam
Where once I gambled like any young lamb
When I walk again by your meadows and springs
I know you my home, for my heart swells and sings ෨

THE BOY JESUS

Who is this child you are holding
With an outpouring of such joy?
What mystery here is unfolding,
What hope do you see in this boy?
Simeon, you were once promised,
The Lord's great salvation to see:
Is this babe you've cradled and kissed
The crux of mankind's destiny?

This boy before you all sitting -
You teachers well versed in the law -
Your cleverness he is outwitting,
His intellect beggars you all.
At barely twelve years he's your master,
His reasoning stalls your debate,
Though all of your knowledge you muster,
You are humbled - or are you irate?

How could a baby so helpless,
Prompt Simeon's outpouring of praise?
Did others there, who bore witness,
In like manner their voices raise?
How could a twelve year old, guileless
The intelligentsia amaze -
Were this Jesus not the one, peerless:
The Light of the World God has raised.[7] &

---

7   Based on Luke 2:25-35 and Luke 2:41-50

THE CRADLING

Had he been deaf, yet still he would have heard
That sweet prophecy, that long promised word.
Had he been blind, yet still he would have sensed
His years of longing fully recompensed.

So long he'd prayed, and practised to discern
God's purposes for Israel - and had learned
To recognise that measured inner voice -
Devotion to it's leading long his choice.

How tenderly the child he cradles now,
How radiant the light upon his brow,
How exultant is his proclamation:
'This child is for the healing of the nations'.

Yet some nearby, on Simeon, look askance
And with their peers exchange a knowing glance -
Their unenlightened hearts cannot perceive
The worship that this child will yet receive.

There's none so blind as those who will not see,
Or deaf, as ears stopped wilfully:
Lord, save me from the ignorance of pride,
In your Spirit, like Simeon, I would hide.[8] ✎

---

8   Based on Luke 2: 25-35

THE COMING OF THE LIGHT

Don't play those Christmas jingles so early in the year,
I can't cope with muzak ringin' in my ear;
It adds nothing to the season of good cheer:
Just sing a carol clear.
The world is too much with us – take flight!
Join with shepherds in the night:
Bow low, bring hearts contrite,
Contemplate the coming of the light.

Spare me those advertisements selling Christmas joys,
For any who will buy, buy, buy, the latest gizmo-toys.
With 'peace of mind insurance' we're pressured to employ:
Peace, such things, destroys.
The world is too much with us – take flight!
Join with shepherds in the night:
Bow low, bring hearts contrite,
Contemplate the coming of the light.

Supermarket trolleys taking Christmas to the car,
Stuffing for the stomach, booze to stock the bar.
A Sally Ann ensemble's singing somewhere off afar:
Of a baby and a star.
The world is too much with us – take flight!
Join with shepherds in the night:
Bow low, bring hearts contrite,
Contemplate the coming of the light.

Two thousand films at Christmas the TV schedules claim,
'More films, less Christmas', arrogantly proclaim!
Insatiable our appetite, we must be entertained:
Is reality so plain?
The world is too much with us – take flight!
Join with shepherds in the night:
Bow low, bring hearts contrite,
Contemplate the coming of the light.

Please, no twinkling lights beneath suburban skies,
Depicting sleighs and reindeer: they are no surprise.
They just don't figure with a stable's dirt & flies.
No more Christmas lies!
The world is too much with us – take flight!
Join with shepherds in the night:
Bow low, bring hearts contrite,
Contemplate the coming of the light. ❧

THE FALL

It is no more, they'll tell you, than the woven web of priests
Of Adam, and Eve, and the serpent - spun to spoil their feasts
They regard as odious, this account of man's first fall
A superstitious fable, set to ensnare us all

To burden us with sinfulness, and so with guilt and shame
We'll define what's good, they say; morality, we'll frame
We'll educate, and regulate - with science at the fore
We'll build a new society free of want and war

Oh, deluded dreamers too rebellious to see
The flaws in human nature writ large through history
Man's inhumanity to man, blights each bloodied page
We are no more enlightened than in any other age

So let us not so readily that old garden dismiss
Or the gardener who still today comes into our midst
Bearing balm most excellent our erring ways to mend
The one who for our benefit his life's blood did spend ∾

(Inspired by a few sentences in the closing pages of *'For The Islands I Sing'*
- the autobiography of George Mackay Brown.)

THE GUITAR (and other stringed instruments)

As these bright strings
In consort ring,
The soul within
Answering sings.

Deep mystery:
How can it be
Vibrating wires
Kindle such fires

Round, profound,
Emotive sound:
Resonant art -
Resounding heart

Above creed or race,
In every place,
This gift cherish -
Or else perish.

Responsive remain
To note and refrain;
Rejoice each day
Being made this way. ❧

THE HAWTHORNE

Along the bough, on every branch
The transformation is complete
In wave on wave, an avalanche
Of snowy petals falling fleet
From crown to toe, from head to feet

The hawthorn's nature was concealed
Its thorny spikes did but mislead
Now its joy is seen revealed
Which winter did a while impede
Now spring's arrived, its mirth is freed

And many other joyous trees
Reach exultant to the skies
Leaves orchestrated by the breeze
The haunt of bees and butterflies
From whose branches birds arise

Lord, I would be as some tall tree
Secure in purpose, unperturbed
By winds of wild philosophy
My roots in you, all undisturbed
My fruit in season seldom curbed ❧

THE OLD INN

The thin smoke from the incandescent fire
Rises past the blackened chimney sides
As though a spirit climbing ever heavenwards
As though a supplication upwards glides

The inn is quiet tonight – deep in winter
Snow is building up about these parts
And regulars, and travellers, and tourists
Are loathe to venture far from their own hearths

For a while the old inn seems so timeless
It might be an age that knew no car
As ghosts of horses whinny in the stables
Ploughmen and drovers jostle in the bar

There upon the burnished wooden settle
A weathered shepherd from a bygone age
Converses with a blacksmith in the corner
With wit and wisdom of the country sage

Though some within were given to indulgence
And would in time a sorry levy pay
For sweat of brow, and labour, and endurance
Old ale is fitting at the eve of day

UNDER THE MERCY

Many in those times practised mercy
Slow to either give or take offence
Caring less for rights, and more for love and duty
A quiet conscience more than recompense

In this welcome absence of distraction
The ambiance of this ancient inn
I feel again a breath of benediction
And my thin smoke ascends from deep within ☙

THE SHOUT

It could have been the end of him, that shout,
When loudly he'd called, 'Lazarus, come out!'
When, deeply moved, he stood before the cave,
Directions for the stone's removal gave,
And with his gaze uplifted to the sky,
For benefit of all those standing by,
He'd thanked his Father who had given leave,
For His empowerment, that all might believe.

Had not the dead man then before them stood,
How surely then would condemnation flood,
Had he remained, still rotting, where he lay,
Then ridicule and malice win the day,
But there stood Lazarus, risen from the dead,
Bound hand and foot, and all around his head:
The power and might of God on earth displayed,
Invested in, and on Jesus laid.

No charlatan, or of delusion led,
No simulation in the tears he shed -
He knew the scene before him all too well,
That in like tomb he too would shortly dwell.
This man of sorrows, familiar of grief,
Would soon grotesquely die with common thief.
By his own people, spat upon and spurned,
Though his great heart, for their forgiveness burned.

It could have been the end, that cross of shame,
Whereon he entered into death's domain,
Enduring unimaginable pain,
Convulsing and disjointing all his frame -
That he might win a name above all names;
That he the victor's crown might yet attain.
For our redemption he, by us, was slain:
The strategies of darkness were in vain.

It could have been the end of him, that tomb -
But his great Father made of it a womb
From which burst forth, apparelled now in light,
The holy Lamb of God upon our sight.
The cloth that round his head had formed a band
Lay folded flat by some angelic hand:
Deep purposes of God that day were gained,
No power on earth can now suppress his name!

THE TEME

The tranquil valley of the Teme
Its water meadows lush and green
With soft autumnal hues serene
Caresses the eye

The rising sun ignites the sky
Aflame the clouds adrift on high
And songbirds lift their heads to cry
As the dawn breaks

On willowed pools the sunlight plays
While flocks beside the river graze
And walkers pause to still their gaze
As swans sail by

Here, as the setting sun goes down
The folk of villages and town
Have warmer smiles and fewer frowns
Less often sigh

The river has a different show
When all is bound with ice and snow
Now slow and silent is its flow
Earth slumber takes

When springtime rains will not abate
Then fearsome is the Teme in spate
Such anger, now its foremost trait
Sea alone slakes ✍

THE WAY

There's majestic music that I love
The power and passion of the symphony
There are melodies pure as whitest dove
And harmonies deeper than the sea

But one song on my spirit ever jars
One song always gives me pain
Recorded by a galaxy of stars
So many who would echo it's refrain

It tells of those, bloodied yet unbowed
Who shake their fists at life, despising shame
They fear not man or God, and cry aloud
'I did it my way', their strident claim

There's a story through the ages told
A garden and a sacred knowledge tree
Of Adam, and how he first took hold
Of it's forbidden fruit, rebelliously

'I did it my way', his remorseful cry
And thus began the tumult of our woes
We wrestle right and wrong, both you and I
Whilst law and regulation ever grows

But there's another story, greater far
Again, one in a garden made a choice
In whose hands and feet outrageous scars
Tell the outcome of the words he voiced

'I'll do it your way', his submission there
Friends heard him weeping in the night
To do another's will was all his care
And so began the rescue from our plight

For Adams fault, and our unruly ways
Were with him nailed upon another tree
He is the new Adam, him all praise
Who by his sacrifice have been set free

There's another music many sing
A swelling chorus, heard in every land
Songs of honour to the Servant-King
From subjects at the Servant-King's command

An ever growing multitude who bow
Then to the Prince of Peace lift their gaze
Who taste of heaven, though on earth below
'We'll do it your way', the great song they raise ❧

THOMAS

They call me Doubting Thomas and I'm worthy of the name,
For I was so reluctant to believe:
To believe Christ the Crucified could win eternal fame
By rising, resurrected, from the grave.
I'd walked with the disciples on the shores of Galilee,
With Peter, James, Matthew, Luke, and John;
I'd seen how Jesus healed the sick, and make the blind to see,
And how his presence like a beacon shone.

But controversy, with Jesus, followed in his wake:
For every devotee, an enemy;
Antagonistic forces sought his blameless life to take,
And soon he hung, accursed, upon a tree.
Then terrible the darkness which fell upon the land
And desolate the hearts of all his friends;
Perplexed and disillusioned, we could not understand
Why he we thought messiah so should end.

Yet some among his followers wildly entertained
A hope - I thought no more than fantasy:
They recalled the master's teaching and how he had claimed
He would demonstrate immortality.
Then excitable women told of an empty tomb
Wherein the corpse of Jesus had been laid;
There to anoint the body, in the early morning gloom,
They'd now returned both joyful and afraid.

UNDER THE MERCY

These overwrought imaginings - rumours, gossip, hopes,
All such remained anathema to me;
His suffering and perishing upon Golgotha's slopes -
This alone the stark reality.
So when told of a gathering behind doors locked and barred,
Where he'd appeared and spoken, 'It is I',
Where he'd displayed his hands, his feet, his side so deeply scarred;
How he'd conversed and eaten with them by,

I raised my eyes to heaven, in exasperation cried,
'Unless I touch the nail holes in his hand,
And place my fist within the void the sword pierced in his side,
I'll not believe - on this I take my stand!'
This stubborn resolution, this propensity to doubt,
Might have blighted and embittered all my days -
Had not the patience of my Lord put all my doubt to rout,
Had not his mercy outweighed my malaise.

For his closest friends and followers, again that same week,
Gathered anxiously behind doors secured,
And I had been prevailed upon to meet with them and seek
Direction, midst upheaval and discord.
And there my bitter scepticism, gently, was excised,
There first I heard the risen Lord's 'Shalom';
For there he stood among us, as the sun stands in the skies,
And there his battle scars I looked upon

And how those scars transfixed my gaze - I see them still today,
Insignia of affliction and of grief;
He bid me touch these weeping wounds, on them my fingers lay:
The wounds he bears for all mankind's relief.
He bid me reach my unclean hand unto his riven side
And place it where the sword had been thrust in;
He bid me soften my hard heart, and cast my doubt aside
And renewed life, believing, begin.

That hour I knew him to be raised the conqueror of death;
Victoriously upon death he had trod:
And something yet more wonderful arrested now my breath,
'My Lord', I cried, 'My Lord and my God'.
For then the import of his scars imprinted on my mind:
Our woes and joys he intimately shares;
The vagaries and suffering so common to mankind,
These too, he experiences and bears.

For he is called 'Our Father'; and his nature is to care -
Such care can never be divorced from pain.
Such parenting is costly: he himself he did not spare,
But gave himself for our eternal gain.
It cost him then at Calvary, it costs him still today:
He grieves for us, as he has ever done;
And weeps to see our foolishness, when we far from him stray -
Like the father of the Prodigal Son.

UNDER THE MERCY

I'm still called Doubting Thomas, to my everlasting shame,
But my Lord, in his mercy, pitied me,
And gave me revelation of the glory of his name
That I might yet his true disciple be.
And still today, my grieving God, to all who truth would seek,
Reveals his nature and his wounds displays:
Great wounds that of his sacrifice and self abasement speak
And mark him worthy of our love and praise. ✎

TRUTH

Schooled in the pride and sophistries of Rome
The discourse of the worldly wise
He'd known his star's ascendant rise
Now governance his hard won prize
But in Jerusalem to make a home?

Oh! 'Subjugated' Israel's anguished cry!
And in his palace Pilate groans
The Jews, obdurate as a stone
Distil their rage on one alone
And come to Pilate crying, 'Crucify!'

And who the object of their bitter spleen?
One in whom no falsehood found
In whom was grace seen to abound
Around whose heart great love was wound
Whose words the wisest ever there has been

Now destiny brings these two face to face
The wielder of Rome's temporal power
And one, foretold, born for his hour
Who wicked forces would devour
Listen what between these two takes place!

'Are you', Pilate asks, 'King of the Jews?'
The one arraigned in court replies
'My poverty my power belies
My Kingdom's hid from this world's eyes

And all my subjects ever Truth pursue'
And once again sad sophistry deceives
His eyebrows raised, Pilate enquires
Yet no enlightenment desires
Of him whose light would men inspire
'What is truth?', he asks, and straightway leaves

Was ever greater irony at play?
The question on which ever turns
Philosophy. For answer yearns
Each generation - each must learn
Yet poor benighted Pilate turns away

Turns from the truth in Christ personified
Who majesty had laid aside
And come to earth, eschewing pride
Gave leave to Pilate to preside
To, 'Innocent', proclaim - yet crucify

Look into the manner of Christ's dying
The words of mercy falling from the cross
Listen for the watchers final sighing
Stricken now with terrible remorse

Hear the verdict of the centurion
'This man, surely, was the Son of God'
Give his claims due consideration
Let not your feet with sophistry be shod[9] ❧

---

9   Base on John 18:38

THE WOMAN AT THE WELL

It had always been a weary business,
Fetching water from old Jacob's well -
The sun above so fierce and pitiless,
The ground so hot whereon my footsteps fell.
Beside the well, his brow upon his hands,
Like one who of some future sorrow knew,
Upon a stone, fatigued as from a journey,
There sat the lonely figure of a Jew.

As I lowered down for the cool water,
Without a word or glance, as though alone,
He spoke - as loving father to a daughter,
No animosity in word or tone.
Yes, a Jew had asked of me a favour,
That of the precious water he might share -
And I, a woman and despised Samaritan!
No prejudice in his demeanour there.

I would ask, he said, for living water,
If I but knew the gift he could impart:
Thirst quenching water, everlasting -
A spring of water welling in the heart.
And though I scarcely followed all his meaning,
Instinctively I knew that it was good:
An end to thirst, and end to all the craving -
And so I asked...at which he smiled and stood.

He touched my arm, and bid me fetch my husband,
And at his touch, I could not hide the truth:
He knew of all my sorrowful liaisons,
He knew of all my waywardness since youth.
He must be, I thought, a holy prophet,
And, colouring beneath his artless gaze,
To deflect his measured observation,
I asked some question of the place for praise.

He answered with such patience and conviction,
In words I did not fully understand,
That brought to mind thoughts of the Messiah,
The one who would explain all God had planned.
Of this I spoke, of this prophetic teaching,
And he, in voice expansive as the sea,
Declared, in words as though from heaven reaching,
'I, that speak unto you now, am he'.

And then, in turmoil and confusion,
I left my pitcher, hastened back to town,
To tell my neighbours all this conversation -
At Jacob's well, had I Messiah found?
In those short years before the crucifixion
I came to know as truth all he declared:
How death was swallowed up in resurrection;
And the living water he with me had shared. ❧

WONDER

It was just a newt, but to my eyes a wonder
And all around that fern fringed woodland pool
Wild things thrived, in dewy splendour
Each leaf and frond and flower, a jewel

The thrush would stall my eager playing
Those cadences of undiluted praise
And as I grew, my eyes to blue hills straying
I loved the silver streams and sunlit days
And in the spring, the bluebells, in confusion
Tumbled down beneath the lofty trees
Spilling their cups in riotous profusion
Upon the passing shoulder of the breeze

Through the wood a brook ran ever singing
Now in shadow, now in liquid light
Mosses to its banks and pebbles clinging
Its murmurings were ever my delight

In the wood the rhododendrons flourished
Their blooms bursting sharp upon the eye
And all this world of woodland, I cherished
It was to me all heaven, earth, and sky

I would return, to taste again such wonder
When my features bore deep marks of time
To find all gone, all torn asunder
Sold and sacrificed to urban design

Though such wonder cannot be recaptured
And ever further from our recall strays
Another wonder now my heart enraptures
A glimpse of heaven's glories in my gaze. ✌

WORSHIP

When I look up to the starry heavens,
Or savour the loveliness of earth,
I'm infused again with awe and wonder
And thankfulness that I was given birth.
When I stand among Your holy people,
Offering my poor impoverished praise,
Your presence delights and consumes me,
And in Your worship I could spend my days.
In worship, arrested by Your holiness,
Our consciences awake to hidden fault;
But we rejoice for You are our redeemer:
Forgiveness, with Your life, for us You bought.

In praise, we celebrate Your truthfulness
And graciousness in all you did and taught;
As we learn to recognise Your beauty,
You refine and purify our thoughts.
With renewed assurance of Your goodness,
From the path set before us we'll not stray,
Gladly submissive to Your purposes,
Your spirit and your word direct our way.
When all is gathered up in adoration,
Our eyes upon the cross of Jesus stayed,
Lost to self, we find ourselves in worship:
For this the very purpose we were made.[10]

---

10   Inspired by William Temple's reflections on the meaning and value of
worship.

First lines

The Author

Pete Hollingsworth

Pete Hollingsworth was born in the Stroudwater valley, becoming an engineering apprentice in a Cotswold village in the 1960s, knowing "little of literature and even less of poetry". In those days, motor cycles preoccupied his energies – along with other pursuits not uncommon among young the young!

Further Education developed his engineering knowledge and (following an overland journey to India in company of some two-hundred university students), he gained a place at teachers training college...and duly began to teach in a Birmingham comprehensive. This was a hugely formative period for a 'country boy' thrust into city life and the rigours of the classroom – "I'd so much to learn!".

Encouraged by a friend to help run holiday camps for schoolchildren during the long summer break, he qualified with the British Canoe Union so as to provide proper care and instruction when taking groups out in kayaks on Lyn Padarn in Snowdonia. Meeting Gill, his wife and moving to lecture in Further Education in Hereford, followed – along with their children, Claire, Gareth, and Paul – proved even more formative.

Now retired, Pete remains active, kayaking, playing tennis, and singing and playing guitar at local folk music sessions. For decades, he and Gill have been active in the local church. Gill's passion is for all things 'Patchwork and Quilting', and their home in a Welsh Marches' cottage displays many examples of her craftsmanship. They greatly enjoy holidays in both the UK and abroad in their small motorhome – in which many of the lyrics and poems here were conceived.

Pete tells how his writing began, "Some years ago, Gill and I were walking the fields and pathways around Nevern – a picturesque village in North Pembrokeshire. Summer breezes and birdsong drifted across the meadows, and sunlight bounced off the ripples of the river winding it's way towards the estuary.

After the walk, and a fresh brew of tea, I strolled into Nevern's old stone church – and found, resting on a deep window ledge, two large books. They were pulpit bibles, one in Welsh, the other English. What I read there changed the course of my life – and led in time to this book. Earlier that same day, I had been scribbling down some words around an idea: that of using Leonard Cohen's extraordinary song 'Hallelujah' as a vehicle telling something of the life of King David – the 'singer/ songwriter' of his day, and the author of many Psalms.

After thirty or so unproductive minutes, I folded my notebook and made a simple prayer, 'Lord, I don't want to waste your time, or mine, if this is not something acceptable to you'. To my shame, I hardly expected an answer – all this took place during a bleak period of doubt and stagnation.

But here, resting on the stone window ledge, appeared an amazing answer: each volume was open to the account of the introduction of David – then an unknown shepherd boy – in the bible narrative, (I Chronicles 16). Within a few days, the revised 'Hallelujah' was completed – and a passion sparked which flamed into these lyrics and poems".

Pete still views this development with some wonder....